The Atmosphere

Illustrations: Janet Moneymaker
Design/Editing: Marjie Bassler

The Atmosphere
ISBN 978-1-953542-18-2

Published by Gravitas Publications Inc.
Imprint: Real Science-4-Kids
www.gravitaspublications.com
www.realscience4kids.com

Take a deep breath.

Now breathe out.

What is it that you are breathing?

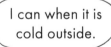
Can you see your breath?

I can when it is cold outside.

The **atmosphere** is the part of Earth that has the air we breathe.

The atmosphere sits on top of Earth's crust and goes up about 60 miles (97 kilometers) above the surface.

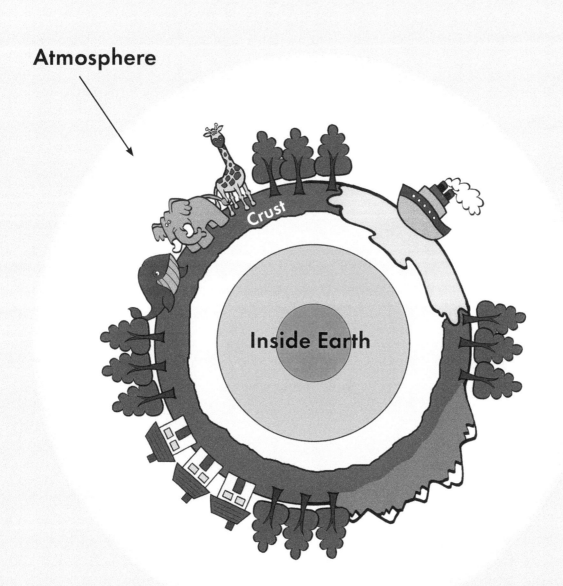

Atmosphere

Crust

Inside Earth

The atmosphere is made up of different gas **molecules**.

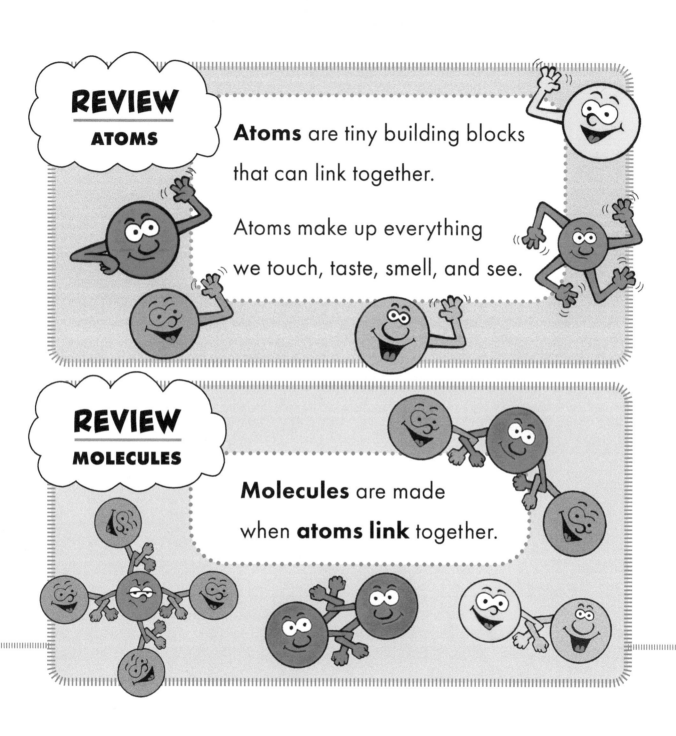

REVIEW
ATOMS

Atoms are tiny building blocks that can link together.

Atoms make up everything we touch, taste, smell, and see.

REVIEW
MOLECULES

Molecules are made when **atoms link** together.

The molecules that make up most of the atmosphere are **nitrogen gas, oxygen gas, carbon dioxide gas,** and **water vapor**.

I did not know there are different molecules in air!

Nitrogen Gas Molecule
(2 nitrogen atoms linked)

Oxygen Gas Molecule
(2 oxygen atoms linked)

Carbon Dioxide Gas Molecule
(1 carbon and 2 oxygen atoms linked)

Water Vapor Molecule
(1 oxygen and 2 hydrogen atoms linked)

All of the gases in the air go inside your **lungs** when you breathe in.

Your body only uses the oxygen gas.
The other gases just go into and out
of your lungs.

My body uses lots of
oxygen when I run.

Your lungs have special **cells** that take the oxygen out of the air so your body can use it to make **energy**.

All living things are made up of **cells**.

Cells are made of **atoms** and **molecules.**

Cells are too tiny to be seen with only your eyes.

Cells work together to do lots of different jobs inside living things.

Weather happens in the atmosphere. Snowstorms, strong winds, rain, **tornadoes**, and **hurricanes** are all types of weather.

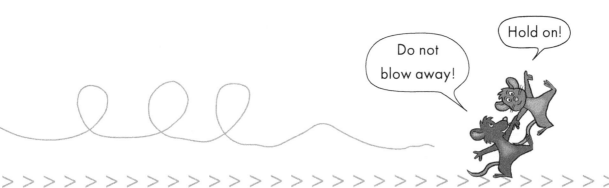

Weather patterns change over time and are different from place to place in the world.

Climate refers to the usual weather patterns in a particular area. For example, a desert is an area that has very little rain or snow.

The atmosphere is very important for life on Earth. We would not be able to live without it.

I am so happy we have air to breathe!

And rain to make things grow!

How to say science words

atmosphere   (AAT-muh-sfeer)

atom   (AA-tum)

carbon dioxide   (CAR-buhn diy-OCK-siyd)

cell   (SEL)

climate   (KLIY-muht)

energy   (E-nuhr-jee)

hurricane   (HUH-ruh-kayn)

hydrogen   (HIY-druh-juhn)

lung   (LUHNG)

molecule   (MAH-lih-kyool)

nitrogen   (NIY-truh-juhn)

oxygen   (OCK-sih-juhn)

science   (SIY-ens)

tornado   (tawr-NAY-doh)

water vapor   (WAH-tuhr VAY-puhr)

weather   (WEH-thuhr)

What questions do you have about THE ATMOSPHERE?

Learn More Real Science!

Complete science curricula from Real Science-4-Kids

Focus On Series

Unit study for elementary and middle school levels

Chemistry
Biology
Physics
Geology
Astronomy

Exploring Science Series

Graded series for levels K–8. Each book contains 4 chapters of:

Chemistry
Biology
Physics
Geology
Astronomy

CPSIA information can be obtained
at www.ICGtesting.com
Printed in the USA
BVHW022237030422
633249BV00015B/496

9 781953 542182